W9-BNS-122

What's Awake?

Opossums

Patricia Whitehouse

Heinemann Library
Chicago, Illinois

© 2003 Reed Educational & Professional Publishing
Published by Heinemann Library,
an imprint of Reed Educational & Professional Publishing,
Chicago, Illinois

Customer Service 888-454-2279
Visit our website at www.heinemannlibrary.com

Designed by Sue Emerson, Heinemann Library
Printed and bound in China

07 06 05 04
10 9 8 7 6 5 4 3 2

Library of Congress Cataloging-in-Publication Data
Whitehouse, Patricia, 1958-
    Opossums / Patricia Whitehouse.
        p. cm. — (What's awake)
Includes index.
Summary: A basic introduction to opossums, including their habitat, diet, and physical features.
    ISBN: 1-58810-880-5 (HC), 1-40340-627-8 (Pbk.)
    1. Opossums—Juvenile literature. [1. Opossums.] I. Title.
QL737.M34 W48 2002
599.2'76—dc21

2001006395

Acknowledgments
The author and publishers are grateful to the following for permission to reproduce copyright material:
p. 4 Steve Strickland/Visuals Unlimited; pp. 5, 9, 16, 22 Joe McDonald/Visuals Unlimited; p. 6 John D. Cunningham/ Visuals Unlimited; pp. 7, 8L S. Maslowski/Visuals Unlimited; p. 8R V. McMillan/Visuals Unlimited; p. 10, 17 J. L. Lepore/ Photo Researchers, Inc.; p. 11 David J. Sams/Stock Boston, Inc./PictureQuest; p. 12 Maslowski/Visuals Unlimited; p. 13 John Mitchell/Photo Researchers, Inc.; p. 14, 20 Jeff Lepore/Photo Researchers, Inc.; p. 15 David Newman/Visuals Unlimited; p. 18 Steve Maslowski/Photo Researchers, Inc. p. 19 Gary Walter/Visuals Unlimited; p. 21 Michael Habicht

Cover photograph by Joe McDonald/Visuals Unlimited

Special thanks to our advisory panel for their help in the preparation of this book:

Eileen Day, Preschool Teacher
Chicago, IL

Ellen Dolmetsch,
Library Media Specialist
Wilmington, DE

Kathleen Gilbert, Teacher
Round Rock, TX

Sandra Gilbert,
Library Media Specialist
Houston, TX

Angela Leeper,
Educational Consultant
North Carolina Department
of Public Instruction
Raleigh, NC

Pam McDonald, Reading Teacher
Winter Springs, FL

Melinda Murphy,
Library Media Specialist
Houston, TX

The publisher would also like to thank Dr. Dennis Radabaugh, Professor of Zoology at Ohio Wesleyan University in Delaware, Ohio, for his help in reviewing the contents of this book.

Some words are shown in bold, **like this.**
You can find them in the picture glossary on page 23.

Contents

What's Awake?

Some animals are awake when you go to sleep.

Animals that stay awake at night are **nocturnal**.

Opossums are awake at night.

What Are Opossums?

Opossums are **marsupials.**

Opossums have a **pouch** for their babies just like this kangaroo.

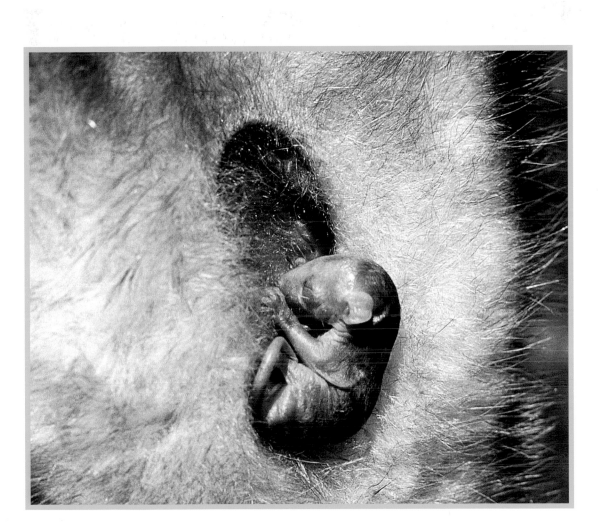

Marsupial babies stay in their mother's pouch while they grow.

What Do Opossums Look Like?

opossum

cat

Opossums are the size of a cat.

They have gray or black **fur**.

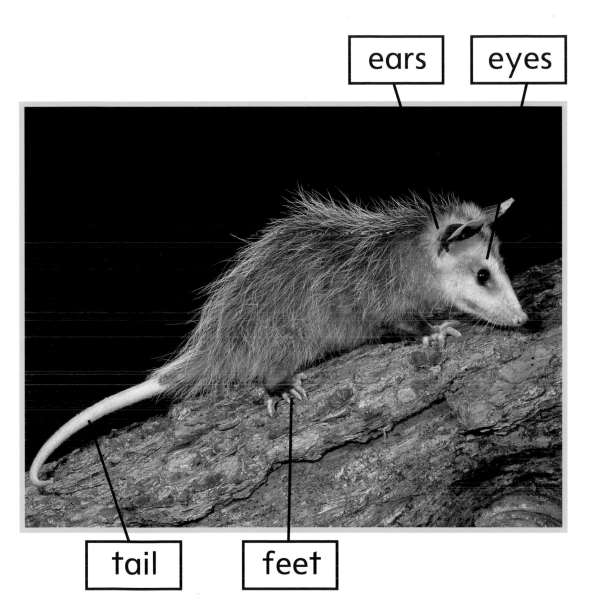

ears eyes

tail feet

Opossums have black eyes and ears.

They have pink feet and pink tails.

Where Do Opossums Live?

In the wild, opossums live in the woods.

They sleep in **dens**.

In the city, opossums live in trees or near houses.

What Do Opossums Do at Night?

Opossums sleep most of the time.

After dark, they come out of their **dens**.

They look for food.

They eat for a few hours
and go back to sleep.

What Do Opossums Eat?

In the wild, opossums eat small animals and bugs.

They eat fruit and leaves.

In the city, opossums eat these things, too.

They also eat food from garbage cans.

What Do Opossums Sound Like?

Opossums are usually very quiet.

Opossums can make a hissing noise.

They do this when they are afraid.

How Are Opossums Special?

Opossums can hang by their tails.

Sometimes they carry their babies on their backs.

Opossums trick animals that try
to eat them.

They play dead until the animal
walks away.

Where Do Opossums Go during the Day?

In the morning, opossums find a safe place.

They build a **nest** of leaves and grass.

Opossums sleep all day.

Opossum Map

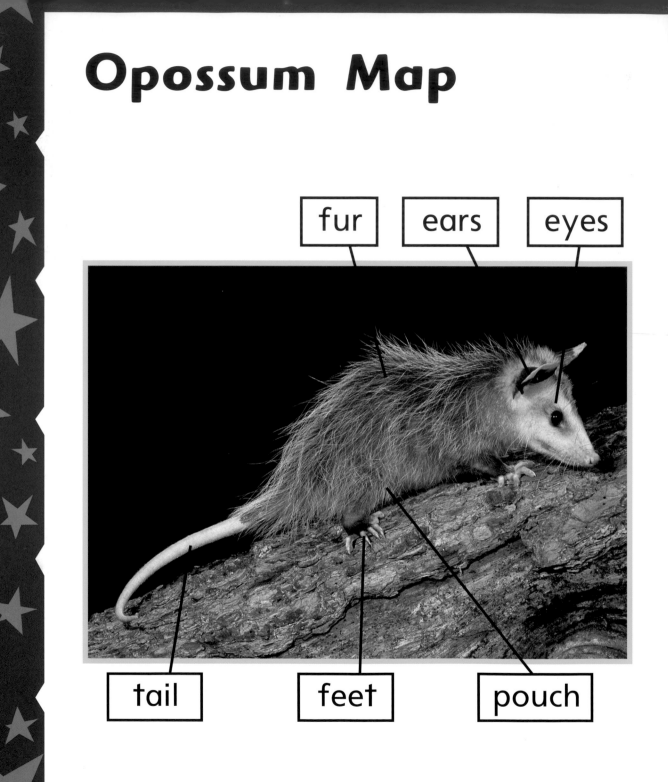

fur ears eyes

tail feet pouch

Picture Glossary

 **den**
pages 10, 12

 **nest**
page 20

 **fur**
page 8

 **nocturnal**
page 4

 **marsupial**
pages 6, 7

 **pouch**
pages 6, 7

Note to Parents and Teachers

Reading for information is an important part of a child's literacy development. Learning begins with a question about something. Help children think of themselves as investigators and researchers by encouraging their questions about the world around them. In this book, the animal is identified as a marsupial. Marsupials are animals that have a pouch in which they nurse and carry their young. The symbol for marsupial in the picture glossary shows baby opossums in their mother's pouch. The symbol for pouch shows the exterior of a kangaroo's pouch with the baby's (joey's) head protruding. Guide children to recognize the difference between mammals and marsupials. Likewise explain that, although kangaroos have the most easily identifiable pouches, other animals—such as opossums—are marsupials, too.

❗ CAUTION: Remind children that it is not a good idea to handle wild animals. Children should wash their hands with soap and water after they touch any animal.

Index